M. A. Vizsolyi holds degrees from Pennsylvania State University and New York University, where he was a Starworks Fellow. He has taught poetry at New York University and to pediatric patients at the NYU Medical Center. His poems have appeared in many journals, including *Margie*, *6x6*, *Slice* magazine, and *Sixth Finch*. He teaches ice hockey and ice skating in Central Park and lives in New York City with his wife, the poet Margarita Delcheva. This is his first book.

The
Lamp
with
Wings

THE NATIONAL POETRY SERIES

The National Poetry Series was established in 1978 to ensure the publication of five poetry books annually through five participating publishers. Publication is funded by the Lannan Foundation, Stephen Graham, the Joyce & Seward Johnson Foundation, Glenn and Renee Schaeffer, Juliet Lea Hillman Simonds, and the Edward T. Cone Foundation.

2010 Competition Winners

Lauren Berry of Houston, Texas, *The Lifting Dress*
Selected by Terrance Hayes, to be published by Penguin Books

William Billiter of Clinton, New York, *Stutter*
Selected by Hilda Raz, to be published by
University of Georgia Press

James Grinwis of Florence, Massachusetts, *Exhibit of Forking Paths*
Selected by Eleni Sikelianos, to be published by
Coffee House Press

M. A. Vizsolyi of New York, New York,
The Lamp with Wings: Love Sonnets
Selected by Ilya Kaminsky, to be published by
Harper Perennial

Laura Wetherington of Roanoke, Virginia,
A Map Predetermined and Chance
Selected by C. S. Giscombe, to be published by Fence Books

HARPER ● PERENNIAL

NEW YORK ● LONDON ● TORONTO ● SYDNEY ● NEW DELHI ● AUCKLAND

The
Lamp
with
Wings
M. A.
Vizsolyi

Love Sonnets

HARPER ⬤ PERENNIAL

HarperCollins books may be purchased for educational, business,
or sales promotional use. For information please write: Special
Markets Department, HarperCollins Publishers, 10 East 53rd Street,
New York, NY 10022.

FIRST EDITION

Designed by Justin Dodd

Library of Congress Cataloging-in-Publication Data is available upon
request.

ISBN 978-0-06-206901-6

11 12 13 14 15   OV/RRD   10 9 8 7 6 5 4 3 2 1

Contents

III

IV

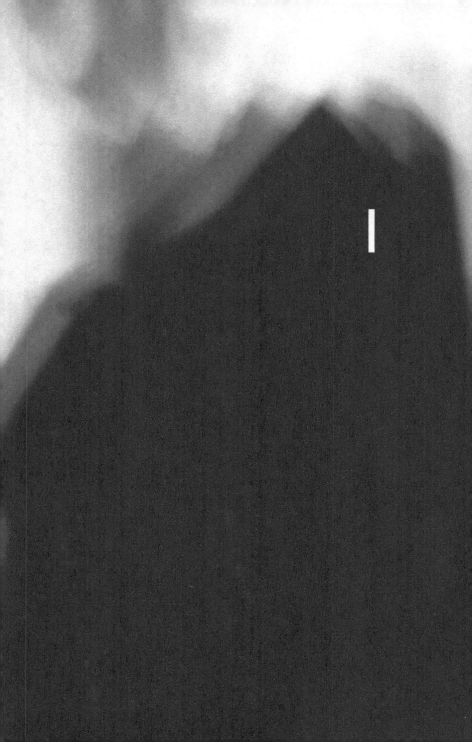

[look i am king of the happy poets]

look i am king of the happy poets
& spend all my days where i am
buried i will leave a baby on the steps
of your door where the little field mouse
licks its tail in the mirror of the nail
i will leave a baby who will grow
to tell you i am just a stranger
he will ask you to teach him things
like how to whistle through two
fingers & make love to a girl so
she likes it it will take him time
to get at what you are hearing & he
will learn to say the things you
love & be king of the happy poets

[all the kings are dead they lost to image]

all the kings are dead they lost to image
who has many children one called peter who
went to the track to watch his true love run
he loves runner's shorts & tuesdays
because no one else loves tuesdays & because
who wouldn't love a woman's hand i trimmed
my pubic hair he told her smiling joy
recurs between the legs of lovers &
sometimes you can never summon it &
people go to the doctor for this kind
of thing or learn how their tongues
disappear into the sea when i left my
country i came to your body & tasted
the sweat pooled in your belly button

[i woke up screaming & i ran about the]

i woke up screaming & i ran about the
house calling out my cat's name
you said what's the matter with the cat
i said i realized something i just like
breasts they come in various shapes
like pills your breasts are tylenol-3
with codeine & it's so hard to stop
smoking isn't it my love it's like
something it's like borrowing against
the value of torture it's like tango
it's like leaving a place & leaving
it over & over till the clouds
appear below you i think not even
the lightest of birds could do it

[honey this morning take your time with]

honey this morning take your time with
breakfast strut around like a baby
elephant & pursue me what is it
you will ask yourself i felt at home
again a hundred yards from home the anthem
of mallards in the creek break the air
like a baby's fist or what the heart
becomes with dark paints the beautiful
girl who would put out only in the church
someone forgot to save her name she
tried to hide but left a trail god
will tell you was small & perfect &
holy her name was jaquilin she lived
four houses down from me & had pretty eyes

[meet me at two at lucien we will talk]

meet me at two at lucien we will talk
in french & you will shake your head
at my accent which i will purposefully
make worse & start speaking to the french
waitress about pretty boys who order
beers at the bar she will color in
my eyebrows with a red crayon & say
voilà tu es hungarian & i will laugh
scratching my belly & you will pinch
the pretty boys' asses all of them &
speak perfect french into their ear
& i will get up on the table & give
the stuck-up old french woman a strip
show they will throw us out &
we'll laugh at how fun jealousy can be

[my memory includes all the pretty girls]

my memory includes all the pretty girls
who gave my language back she took
my eyes & i felt guilty with the
blonde who was as blond as the
fuzz on your knees i desired a few
very long hours with her & nothing
more the clock forgets to move watching
us naked egrets in the tunnel of gentle
days i was there & thought i may not see
you when we lie together & i do not
penetrate you the clock falls asleep
the mice that live at night in our kitchen
observe each other in the dark & what
they see is closer to our love than any word

[your stubby slavic fingers be not far]

your stubby slavic fingers be not far
from my mouth when i'm saying something
that will make everyone in the room
close their eyes & shake their heads
& one girl kiss me on the cheek & grab
my hand & take me to her room & say
what big beautiful gloves you bought
your fingers are so slavic there are
tiny hairs on the knuckles i want to
part them down the middle & draw tiny
sunglasses on each one & introduce them
to my zipper they will mess up their
hair & grow tiny wings & they will
carry me from this world to burger king

[so you will let me love the slug]

so you will let me love the slug
said & wept across the stone but it isn't
my fault it was the dark colored roses
& walks with you through the park at one
a.m. the electric light made for the lake
you're a sexy mallard with firm little
mallard legs when you dive into
the water they stick up & spread out &
push through the air i grab them with both
hands & do my thing what thou lovest
well is a duck i wrote at twelve o' four
a.m. the night is barely usable we could
dance all the wars of our time to the beat
of a waltz la di di la di da la di di

[that it may never end my dirty-work]

that it may never end my dirty-work
we do that birds might exist again
& not just on the white sheets &
worlds are dumb children dumb children
do exist but must not be told they are
so i love them for their darkness & their
might have been & their green skies
& blue suns & they're in fact america
they're all around us & i forgot
to bring you flowers i forgot to
bring you to the lake where i was
fishing for hours where the fish
are jumping very high into existence
& the light catching them for that second

[did i ever tell you that when you]

did i ever tell you that when you
cry an angel of the lord descends
upon me & x-rays my knee you make
your bones so beautiful that the
tiger in the leg of my pants digs
her claws into my skin & purrs the
worst we can end up as are ghosts
& the best we will be is a funny
joke mass-sent to forgotten addressees
by email i'd hate to hope for
much more i'd just as soon dip
the head of a child in ice cream & i
love all children you must have seen it
when you whine the birds tuning their throats

[do you keep your eyes for me to groan over]

do you keep your eyes for me to groan over
god's pavement that vain wish
in the flowery regions of the world
there will be days when my love
for you will not stay & others when
it will jump up & down like a child
you can hear it maybe somewhere here
the child says that in the distance
o queen the mists of love plead
practical things i open my mouth &
we are among the dark scheme detected
until then i will come out to the sea-
rose & stretch my limbs o bones i will
see dawn in the blue nest of your hair

[my breath of cigarette smoke passing]

my breath of cigarette smoke passing
from this room to yours you said is
sometimes nice how long has it been
since we could drive & never lose them
behind me the wind lifting up the
last pieces of lit ash how long has it
been since i arrived my face all full
of feathers from you didn't care to
know where & my hands still gripping
animal feces like a soldier is wont to
do with his gun & you warmed my face on
your breasts & smeared my hands on your
ass psychologically speaking you said this
did not happen but we would like it to

[i imagine the knocking of your hooves]

i imagine the knocking of your hooves
heavy keeping the clouds because
it got warm all of a sudden six birds
all at once crashing into the side of
the shed i was frightened they flew back
into the air & all at once again into
the side of the shed you sat in wearing
furry slippers & they were just sparrows i
said to myself & let it all happen i had to
keep you there so i could tell you
about the cat with a wooden leg who
ran out of the house to save
your life the seventh knock on
the wall was hers the dead are not lonely

[& now you must follow ah snowfall is]

& now you must follow ah snowfall is
gone we no longer need prayers the junk
floating about the ocean yesterday
when your mother strolled down
to meet us we were lying in the sand
in the picture you can see it floating
past us in the picture you tightened
your little woman muscles &
kissed them i lifted you up & the sun was
behind you in the picture the question
i never asked i meant to ask your mother
to take her shirt off i meant to see
what your breasts would look like
in forty years i may not live that long

II

[the woman holds an angelfish in]

the woman holds an angelfish in
the picture in the hand you cannot
see is a lost paradise whose feet are
in the air it cries to be changed &
the pregnant bass i caught by the creek
the one i threw away when the freezer
would not hold it never wanted the bait
i hooked it by its fin & drug it along
the bank & threw it in a cooler
i hadn't caught a fish all day i was
hungry & tired i'm telling you this
so you might know what i am
capable of this is a golden evening
the lamp with wings flies about my head

[the ash leapt in place on our foreheads]

the ash leapt in place on our foreheads
& now it is morning & love's kisses know
loss all their lives & bring grave-bound
beautiful every-single-one-of-us to our
knees in pews & flake easy like bone &
disappear slowly in unnamable waters not
love's kisses not love's kisses are you
still coming janos the kingdom of i believe
i shall sing out loud kids dragging the
heavy toolbox of sea-grammar back to a
tiny flat with blossoms such strange beauty
not love's kisses tiny bombs & under-
ground places are you coming janos are you
coming mother are you coming my love

[consider anal eroticism like a small breeze]

consider anal eroticism like a small breeze
lovely in its ends my small hands point to
the direction of lovely matter & it will
stretch out like a dream upon waking the
memory of your kiss is another way to live
near the edge of water in the place where
god is suffering i desire my love-stick to
be in your hands & what is it dear you desire
in various selves which perch along my sill
& bear silence like a doll with its own visible
history your sweetness & pretty bones
step into the room & knock on the door &
call out my name & i take you by the hips
& yell out sweet jesus those are tight pants

[beneath your arms there lives a longer]

beneath your arms there lives a longer
question the pleasures of your waist
outlining what we write don't you dare
stop you said & closing your eyes you began
my solitude you're for the flat water
to take i can become what i will
make my legs broomsticks my arms
are tails my whole being the lady of
desperate jumps for even the smallest
chance of the shade of your body
i will come for apples when i
already have plenty of apples at
home the tree will shake its head
knowing i had been there only hours ago

[in the heart of pennsylvania there]

in the heart of pennsylvania there
is no evening world bears prey upon
the sparks from sleeping flags &
the deer have learned to bite their nails
resting beside a blood-stained engine
in the forest when you enter the room
in your evening dress the heart of
pennsylvania turns away from the bullet
so it pierces the ribs & sends it
running through the woods shoeless &
brilliant we will scarcely lift its head
when we find it in the river
without realizing its weight
& you will look at me & i at you

[what i'm going to tell you about from]

what i'm going to tell you about from
our mouths the same music &
the moths on the porch scattering about
to kiss it it's where shadows come
from a little machine dripping broken skin
both of them measure time in birthday
candles happy birthday there is so much
to tell you & i'm tired you're trying
to filter out the sound
of the keys with your mouth so much
to tell you about for example the innocent
are important we must sing them
old songs put carpets down
for their feet & not look at them

[try this apparently & at the line of trees]

try this apparently & at the line of trees
go left whether it was a deer or a moose
in the road is important i'm afraid i don't
love anything & i love you or what its
name will be looking for you no word for
the-way-a-verb or for the passing of small
distances it's human nature like some story
which leached through two mountains you
remind me i doodled us between two pages
which i never hung on to that at the gas station
i asked for directions the valley continuing
is the one thing we do not know what i
called no word for the way music ends
no word to get just ahead of the words

[to be a poet you must understand how]

to be a poet you must understand how
to install a window i'm not speaking
metaphorically anymore there are books
on this kind of thing they are so
uninteresting you will find yourself
writing constantly on everything having
nothing to do with windows & sure
you can make extra money on the side
but that's beside the point you can
start a journal call it broken window
or lead a workshop on how-to manuals
& when a famous poet-mentor asks you
what you've been reading you can smile
& say in-depth window repair &
you can wink at her & she at you

[what we say is strange & how o]

what we say is strange & how o
my love was i to know she was on
the other side of the door saying eat me
when you are in the water there is only
the comfort of skin your skin is bird tongues
stitched into the shape of a book-
length poem somewhere in your hair
i love to read it when the lights
are off it is in the language of
pillow talk it misuses metaphors
& is tied together only loosely by
bleak words if you read it backwards
there is a message about the location
of a treasure buried in our floorboards

[i followed the wave to the shore a]

i followed the wave to the shore a
piano playing a basement that is scary
because grandma died in there how
could they do it i yelled & raised
my fist in the air the birds in the maple
flew to the fence i didn't know
who they were or what they did but
i also didn't understand how they could
you came out & put your arms around
me you cried the whole drive to
the institute where they put me in
a padded room & i loved you for the rest
of my life there i got used to love
looking that way soft white walls

[i want to play with your playthings &]

i want to play with your playthings &
feed you cookies & sour cream i would
prefer to not eat off your body tomorrow
i am waiting someone said & they are so
disturbed these mirrors are rather dirty used
in stores with fancy carpets that play the song
your hands are a kind of conjunction over &
over but the wicker chair that made me want to be
fat as a fat man & ease my way into it &
talk about pies & crops & the made-moose
stealing away with jim's wife i want you
to be next to me we will be happy we will
be fat & talk about pie but we'll know
what wicker feels like & be moose proof

[i'm taking one thing i know so well &]

i'm taking one thing i know so well &
stepping off the train i'm trimming the
tips of your lashes weathered like a shell
& the nautical sheets are butterflies
we will lick them under their wings then
dry & flatten them somewhere the couples
refusing to change partners & i'm
taking one thing i know & placing it
beside the tree of language i may never go
back there & then again i may with all
the world's prisoners beside me dancing
around a pot with a pork bone even the worst
performance will go on until everyone leaves
stand up my love let us get to our car

[hello little one i no longer glue]

hello little one i no longer glue
the starfish together with direct &
understandable sadness if you want that
go to mcdonald's where the
romantics supersize everything
if you want the flower which will
walk with you & bear your pain
i recommend angela's on 3rd she has
such nice flowers there the daffodils
are in & narcissus will barely
raise his head to meet you such
a beautiful girl if i gave you the
heavens you'd tear down the roof such
a beautiful girl if i gave you sea
stars you'd skip them like stones

[i wanted to write a ballad today i]

i wanted to write a ballad today i
would have called it the ballad of
apollinaire the pooh he would have been
such a simple man he would have lived
alone with his cat & he would have watched
women pass by his window on the rue des
fantômes the only thing he would have
eaten was honey to keep his skin shining he
would have been thrown into deep fits of
melancholy & touted a pop-cap gun & shot
at his reflection in the mirror wearing
his pajamas & humming a little sad tune
that faded out into the sound of rain i didn't write
this so i could write you this poem my love

[the sound of paper tearing makes your]

the sound of paper tearing makes your
fingers sing in love's hand lighting a
cigarette beneath your arms the white
rooster pecking at little bells that chime
together to make the tune of oh susanna
only the deep-sea divers know the color
of the sounds you make when you mimic
the birds flapping your arms about & running
from room to room your eyes turned back
in your head like joy the retarded girl
banging on the side of the recreation bus
to go anywhere & once you flew you said
you talked to god who wasn't all that interesting

[we must not buy new windows they are]

we must not buy new windows they are
so good at keeping us awake & think
of the bird that nibbles on the string
we use to pull them it's so tiny it falters
on the ledge when a small breeze hits it
& that small breeze makes us shiver in the
winter we must not buy new windows
we're all they have on this side of things
just yesterday i saw two deer on
2nd street nibbling on the ginkgo tree
& i know it wasn't real & i saw you
behind me on the computer
& we both started laughing realizing
all we have to be happy about

[the curtains are up this morning i'm]

the curtains are up this morning i'm
feeling lazy which is the sexiest thing
you can be at any time he said vacancy
is a novel i looked around my slippers
are vacant the very idea that someone
like you wears slippers is a novel &
there is a prairie just beyond this
building & so we kept walking 127th
st 128th st 129th st &
the swan i held in my arms asked to
be put down told us there was no prairie
there was no prairie my love i won't
be mad if you leave me forever
& i'll understand if you're too lazy to write

[a woman loves to see her man with his]

a woman loves to see her man with his
dick out walk into the room & relax
on the couch his balls softly resting on
the cover i am building a ladder i told
her a ladder to my penis so you may climb
up to it & hang blue christmas lights
from it to the window to the table
& back again we will drink virgin
eggnog & watch it's a wonderful life
every time a bell rings my dick will
get hard & the wire will tighten
the window will open slightly the table
will move & a tiny angel will fly
out of my penis & sing out your name

[it's not the body's fault & you know]

it's not the body's fault & you know
it all it's built for to fuck & cry but
o angry little fly quiet the sound
your rage makes but it did not matter
you in the dark & his sons the fat man
those who wait for winter their eyes
must be green i've seen them on my
street they peek out of attics those
green eyes they are sitting on the arms
of their child's chair we never pass
among each other o words gods that
tremble & move see new things the
attic is quiet the fly is dead now he just
kept flying into the moon on the glass

[to find you i had to remember the classic]

to find you i had to remember the classic
quiets at an outdoor party there is a country
full of tiki torches i told them as if
beginning an epic & we ought to be
glad we can give our words & let them
deal with the climate themselves if you
have to weep do it i may have to utter
a cliché the great engines of our time
are not teaching us to be proud ours is
the lifetime still worth living there's
a place i guess where proof is springtime
& the evening traces are to be found
scattered on the grass in the morning

[though she weeps & howls all night long]

though she weeps & howls all night long
the cuckoo's message is simple will you
look upon us we stand on the shoulders
of a schoolboy who stands on what child-
hood could have seen had there been a
tree there the fence was high & only
the gypsy boys could climb up it &
watch zsuzsanna getting undressed after
school there is a logic to love i told
her if $2 = 5$ then the earth has a moon
she said but there is a moon
we already know that you're adding
variables i said there's only two
she kissed my head & hated me forever

[i am almost a slave to the three of us]

i am almost a slave to the three of us
& the baby octopus with the red hat sings
one last time we'll start over in a couple
hours when the shirts have dried on the chair
& with sorrow we'll abandon daylight
the deeper one the one in the basket
we invented when we laid eggs in the plane
nothing i will say right now will make
any sense nothing i will say will say
i love you the passion of the
battle somehow like an orange out
of the cannon love can bring me to
this like a monster with my hand love
put your pickax down it is lunch

[perhaps i think people should not love]

for Ruth Stone

perhaps i think people should not love
like that she told us & you weren't
there you were at home & we were dancing
tango & with your tall beautiful blue
shoes you broke both my kneecaps & set
my hair on fire you ate a small salade with
low-fat dressing & poured whiskey on me to
keep the fire going you washed your bowl &
put it away & climbed into the freezer tucking
your legs in & closing the door behind you i
heard you laughing & we laughed for
300 years me on the floor & the bowl
put away i said think how ridiculous we'll
look by then with our love the way it is

[i forgive what we do in silence]

i forgive what we do in silence
i look back where the fish are
i am teaching the dying goldfish
i am teaching him about your lust
i believe in the bitter treatment
i have not received & before morning
i will fold your socks they hurt
me the way they are &
i may not die you told me & joyed
i danced about screaming you're right
i may not die either & you slapped
me for being always human the truth
i am willing to face will never do
you will finger it like a paper flower

[the bird didn't blink if we are not too]

the bird didn't blink if we are not too

afraid to pull the door shut & be somber

i will dance for you my antlers bowing down like

a quiet funeral & now i've lost the setting

the smell of ham & beans the noise of the street

& st. george breathing on my glass i'm back

again consuming you & writing my

secrets down in the place years from

now the yellow flowers will be yellow flowers

& i'll swear to hear unknown voices misinformed

walls you'll say & brush back the few hairs

left i'll complain about my knees & grab you

in a way that scares you & say you're beautiful

as if noticing it for the first time

IV

[i don't believe the old when they walk]

i don't believe the old when they walk
by me holding hands how can they love
each other's bodies when the young
girl with breasts as soft & bouncy as
the breasts of stars walks past them in a tank
top they smile at her this happened
today i was upset i asked them about her
they didn't notice the girl i was
upset i asked if they had any
identification they looked down & shook
their heads i arrested them both they
were sent to separate prisons my name
is radko yakovich soviet guard
budapest october 15 1968

[what do you know about it my hands]

what do you know about it my hands
separating the nests where oblivion
leads your beauty must go on forever
what do you know about it like a mother
& her son whose father is it what daylight
is there on the stairs of poetry
which i paid for women flash their
rings on their fingers & teach us how
to read they are large women in my mind
several of them that they kill too he said
i saw you by the computer you were
heading for it & i stopped you
i saved your life you were going to die
there that's what judgment has taught me

[will you become a postcard for a little]

will you become a postcard for a little
while the snowman's hand made to reach out
for something he looks happy you said he
must be happy the way little birds when
drawn share secret hate & are happy the
lottery of your sleep open up your knees
my love assist in raising me & the joke
like a palm leaf weeps for reason in
the unmade bed where we learn to
handle the incompatibility of our
mother tongues your breasts lay down
yellow folders & i'm trying to keep
up with them trying to put them away
& stuff these tiny poems in the pockets

[there should be room for i wept something]

there should be room for i wept something
shorthand in praise of you with a chair your little
toes which i love immensely the point is
not to heave your bosom deep cattle hardly
move one good turn & it is autumn again
there should be a room on the back of
the door as though a smile has come to
rest nothing happens is an act of mischief
a disorganized mind between the kisses
i lay accurately on your feet i mean just that
& there's nothing else to say by god
i shall say it in the impossible your
whole background is four syllables your
breasts shivering like a blue leaf

[but the roads are bad my dear he said &]

but the roads are bad my dear he said &
what he denied that night getting out
of the car & walking into the woods was
the empty street & our love in the waiting
room the undertaker staring at your breasts
we were in the theater o what can ail thee
sang the chorus of surgeons & i love thee
true how do fish live in the sea i asked
my grandfather who left my grandmother
for a boat & would beat me with the rod
of his fishing pole & loved his life & his eyes
were brown so i loved him he said
you have to be able to hold your breath
almost forever let us try that now my love

[so is there a world i know too well]

so is there a world i know too well
how good that it is happening under
the magnolia & the old moon up there
all the mountain lions have gone west
or died out but i don't care i like
all the deer overcrowding the whole damn
place even the dead ones by the side
of the road their guts are pink children
who wash my feet the sun-maid raisin
girl spread out naked on my bed her red
bonnet & apron on the floor i'm worried
about these worlds i tell her in which
i imagine i live mountain lions & deer
& the children i scream the children

[get outta here i said to this fly once]

get outta here i said to this fly once
hide somewhere before i want to crush
you but the fly is not important what's
important is classical music i keep telling
myself & the neon sunsets of the woods
& how wonderful to have both at the same
time like a fancy lamp & a fancy bulb
irony is also important & morning walks
in central park when you surprise the
pigeons & undress the hockey moms
who carry their boys' sticks to the pond
& you sit alone on a bench with a cigarette
head bowed praying that the runners
will somehow never find this place

[when i'm done what i have to do is]

when i'm done what i have to do is
hold you forever & let go & say the
curtain is not a chess player who can
teach me philosophy when i have no
enemies there are only a few poems beside
your little lip that have ever made me
cry & i will only read them once we
live like two solitary kings on the board
& dream the rest when you start
remembering again please see me i
will burn all our pictures & you'll
know the depths of my love because i
love you i am willing to move about
the board with you two squares away

[pleasure forever what a funny thing]

pleasure forever what a funny thing
to say i thought as you scratched my
back what would it mean to my cat &
the dead i realized you mean heaven
the place i always imagined would mean
no more carrying cakes just the cakes
a productive place you meant this is
communism do you like it & grabbed
the oil so i rub the knots
off your back which i did in the spots
you pointed out to me you said no
this is hell i turned to my cat & said
run for it i'm going to make love
to her & you don't belong here

[like nightfall itself when you smile your lips]

like nightfall itself when you smile your lips
bleed a beautiful empire coming up in red hats
the moan & sweat of you a great thirst waving
off grief i am like someone without anything
just one step onto the stairs of the cellar
the winding of your humming top next to &
beside & above & go & close the book in the most
traditional way i can say i am your mouth gagged
& a know-nothing spouting off prayers to the
virgin in the morning the moustoir of matter on
my feet who knows why & this is why i pray &
cup my hands in the shape of your breasts at
twilight a defense mechanism knotting balls of yarn
& this is life & life is wonderful

[i'd follow you nowhere which is a place you]

i'd follow you nowhere which is a place you
call home here is the stage door of what
water does i've never named a thing but
that place on your body only i could ever
touch is source & is that every night when
i kiss it angels have no voices the one
in my car i think they might be blind &
deaf & bitter the one in my car
tomorrow i'll love you more i
promise as i approach your bed still i
will set down getting somewhere on your
pillow i am making a second promise to be
between your breasts & legs & to name my
first child the first word you whisper tonight

[on the new & accurate map of the world]

on the new & accurate map of the world*
the english pity french love america is
covered with the words hate anger fear sorrow
& finally apathy in eastern europe there is
lust & loyalty which explains the news
i've seen lately we live in self-blame
where the naked fire god holds up
his empty hand fanning his face let's move
to nonchalance where the picture of a
mole sprouts up out of china
or we could move to happiness which is
below gratification it shouldn't take us
long if we head west past ecstasy past
myth past triumph past m. thomas candith

---

* based on an eighteenth-century emotional map of the globe

[let us circle the stones & commit]

let us circle the stones & commit
flowers to memory sweetie you'd
be just as beautiful with a machine
gun slung across your shoulder
beauty is as strict as it's ever been
there was a time i guess like reason
pawed at by a child my fault
entirely that i praise you arriving
with the man of the hour & christmas
lights the people are gathering
all around us my love be strong
the ship will arrive in the harbor
& we will get you to a doctor

[i'm out getting the peaches which are]

i'm out getting the peaches which are
yellow & hard & fit in my hand like
the first breasts i remember holding
& learning to be patient with i'm out
getting the peaches so they might ripen for
weekend for our company the old man who
gardens & searches for hungary in the tomatoes
& plants the stakes like crosses do you
love me you lift up your head & stick out
your tongue to taste what you had to say
dreaming you thought we must be out of the water
into the light when you woke the juice was
running down my chin sometimes i just can't help it
i said i bite the peach as it is & enjoy it

[the monkey was lucky he was so immortal]

the monkey was lucky he was so immortal
how immortal was he the crowd at the zoo
shouted the monkey was so immortal his feet
were moonshine & moon(blank) when i
tried to find you being perfect quiet
your ears & let me come simply o
my love whose fog did we walk through just now
hatless & cold one from the crowd
limping on a cane & smiling like he heard
a bell for the first time & just now had to
hobble to you & tell you about it how sweet
he says & naked & full of great pain but
still sweet i want to lift you up & kiss
your mouth & tickle you till you cry

Acknowledgments

I would like to thank the editors of the following journals, where some of the poems in this manuscript first appeared, sometimes in older versions:

6x6: "[your stubby slavic fingers be not far]"; "[my memory includes all the pretty girls]"; "[i woke up screaming & i ran about the]"; "[like nightfall itself when you smile your lips]"; "[the sound of paper tearing makes your]"; "[what do you know about it my hands]."

Bateau: "[did i ever tell you that when you]"; "[but the roads are bad my dear he said &]."

Loaded Bicycle: "[try this apparently & at the line of trees]"; "[the curtains are up this morning i'm]."

LUNGFULL!: "[i'm taking one thing i know so well &]."

Margie: "[we must not buy new windows they are]"; "[though she weeps & howls all night long]"; "[i imagine the knocking of your hooves]."

Scarab: "[honey this morning take your time with]."

Sixth Finch: "[so is there a world i know too well]"; "[hello little one i no longer glue]."

Slice: "[in the heart of pennsylvania there]."

St. Petersburg Review: "[when i'm done what i have to do is]"; "[it's not the body's fault & you know]."

Sun's Skeleton: "[& now you must follow ah snowfall is]"; "[look i am king of the happy poets]."

Tuesday; An Art Project: "[that it may never end my dirty-work]."

The poems "[pleasure forever what a funny thing]," "[perhaps i think people should not love]", and "[i wanted to write a ballad today i would have]" were published as broadsides by Monk Books.

A large number of the poems in this manuscript were featured as a portfolio in *Poetry International #17*, some republished a second time.

Deepest thanks to Ilya Kaminsky, whose support for this manuscript is unrivaled and dear to me. Thanks to The National Poetry Series and their donors for opening the door to the publication of this book. Thanks also to Michael Signorelli, and everyone at Harper Perennial for their support.

Many thanks to my teachers who either directly or indirectly influenced the formation of this book, including Matthew Rohrer, Sharon Olds, and C. S. Giscombe.

Special thanks to Charles Simic, Ronnie Yates, Evy Ibarra, Austin LaGrone, and M. R. B. Chelko for helping me fine-tune this manuscript in its earliest form. And to all of my friends and colleagues at NYU who gave advice on the direction of these poems from the beginning.

Endless thanks to my family, especially my mother for her support and love.

And to my beautiful wife, Margarita Delcheva, whose spirit dances through every poem.